BLEEDING ELEGIES

Demons Shattering My Sanity

IANUSI

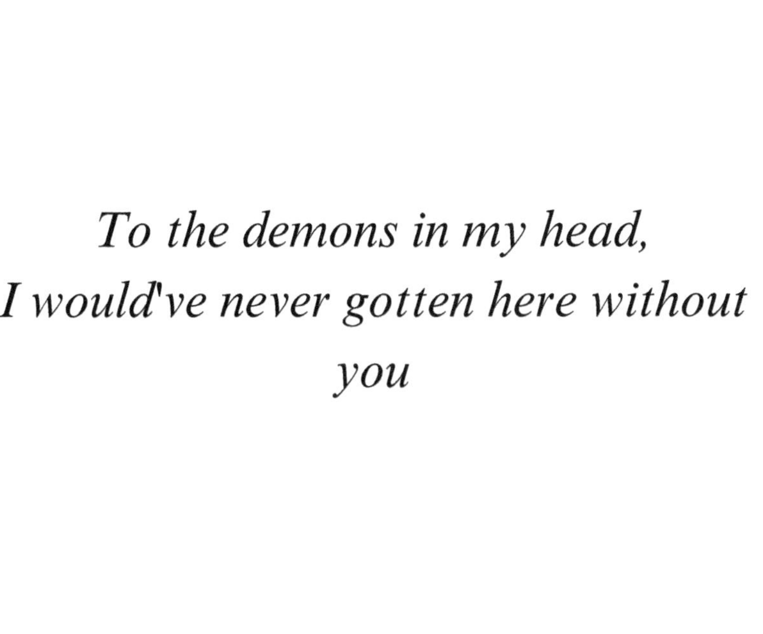

To the demons in my head,
I would've never gotten here without you

PART 1:

DEMONS SHATTERING MY SANITY

The fire is raging red tonight

1

I am exhausted
From listening to people say how
time heals all wounds
And makes it all better
For it does not.
Years ago maybe I did have a heart
But something crushed it
And ever since then,
The bulb has been out.
No matter how long I wait
I can't feel the light in me
No matter how much I try
All I can do is burn, never shine.
Time
Time can heal no wounds.

11

Time takes away what you call the right
To grieve over what you lost that night
A month of mourning, maybe a year
Later, you have to lie and say ‘It doesn’t
affect me’,

III

There are times when you want to plunge
the knife so deep
It tears your emotions apart and kills the
pain
It tears your soul apart and sets you on fire
You want the physical pain so badly
That you can convince yourself that the
tears are not cause you are breaking apart
At least not emotionally.

IV

Winters
Winters are beautiful for everything is dead
You look around and find that for once
You aren't the only one lifeless
You can scar your skin and have a reason to wear full sleeves
You can shiver and feel free
You can dance and hum and sing
And hide even outside
For no one will ever see
Winters are so beautiful indeed.

A vase to your head
Is perhaps the only thing
That will make you regret
What you did to me
In love's stead.
Tying you up and making you bleed
Is perhaps the only way
To make you see
The damage you did to me.
The screams die in my throat
As you walk away with no remorse
Carrying the pieces of my soul.

VI

Isn't it pretty how
People cut down
The pretty wings
And curse at the bird
For the heights it couldn't reach.
People break and break
Later throw words away
At the pretty little thing
Tumbling astray.

VII

I wonder how falling in love feels like
For it is hard to come by.
I wonder whether it happens in the blink of
an eye
Or slowly builds up as the time passes by.
I wonder whether it makes you lie
Or lose your mind.
I wonder if it makes you kill
To keep them alive.
Is it shortness of breath
Or peace of mind?
A flutter in the gut
Or warmth deep inside?
Does your heart beat faster
Or the pace even out?
I wonder if it matters to me

I wonder if it matters to me
If the ink diffuses
Or the nib sinks
Through my soul
For I'll forever be
Undone by you,
Made only for me.

VIII

People took and took
The light in me
Then doused the star
Burning in deep
Look into my eyes
And the demons howling
Buried in me
Then wonder and ask
Why the smile is hollow
And when I sink my teeth low
They bleed and ask
What did they do
To deserve a beast like me

IX

Sh...keep that tarp closed
When they ask look down
Don't let the remains of your soul
Escape from your mouth.
Hide your shattered heart
Show your docile mind
Keep that rage deep inside.

You can cry
You can bleed
You can be
No one will ever see.
As long as you keep it deep inside
Cover up the blood
Hide the scars
And burn yourself so bright
The light hides the stars
Fleeting in the dark night.
For they are not specs of light
But demons planning to kill you tonight.

The fire is me tonight

PART 2:

SHADOWING HAUNTING MY MIND

Maana ke hum yaar nahin
Lo tay hai ke pyaar nahin
Phir bhi nazrein na tum milaana
Dil ka aitbaar nahi

1

I moulded myself
To write like you
To speak like you
To act like you
To love what you did
To throw what you didn't
To make sure that every time you
looked at me
You saw a home, you saw yourself.
Only to find out that you hated
yourself.

11

In another life
Perhaps we work
Perhaps we rhyme
Perhaps we love
At the same time.
Perhaps we hope
Perhaps we pray
Perhaps we don’t
Set flowers on our own grave.
Perhaps we match
The rhymes of our heart
Perhaps we become more than just art.

III

I find a muse every time you break my heart
Only to feel you in every spark
They might be the blood that runs through my veins
And blood changes
But you are my heart
And the heart is always the same.

IV

I always wanted them to write a book
On the broken boy
And the girl who loved too much
I always wanted them to make a song
On the devil
And the angel who was hurting too much
I always wanted to see poems
On the guy who killed
And the girl who died for love.
Yet I was in an unmarked grave
But the dedication to every tragedy ever written.
They did write a book
They did make a song
I did see the poem
But they failed to be what I was hoping for
Just like you.

I think I imagine you
Holding the railing of the balcony
In the middle of the night
While staring at the only source of light
Miles away
Watching me
And wondering
About what exactly you did wrong
I imagine you beating yourself up
While you see me dance with him
But instead, there's no him
And I am watching you
From miles away
Carrying her on your back
Waiting for you to come back
Wondering where I went wrong
Because when I left

You didn't pursue me
You replaced me
In your heart
And in your home

VI

I was so sure that we'd be forever
That I forgot to have a proof
That we existed
I think 60 years later
When I tell my grandkids about you
They'll think that I am crazy
And I think that I am crazy too
Because I took out the shattered pieces of my heart
To fill in the missing spaces of yours
But how will I ever convince them
That even though you loved her
Your heart
Is mine.
Quite literally so.

VII

I never used to believe
That love and hate could go together
Until I read of Jacks of Hollow
And thought of you
And then read of Ryle
And thought of you again.

VIII

At first, there was only darkness,
Only you, only me
But we ventured out to find
Our stars, our light
And then,
There was only loneliness.

IX

I think that heartbreak
Is the worst tragedy
Misfortune is up to fate
Death is up to 'God'
But heartbreak
Heartbreak is deliberate
And that is why
It hurts the most

You ruined me
For every sunset
Ever dip
Every margherita I'll ever sip
Every movie reminds me
Of our date
Every coffee reminds me
Of our game
I am utterly, truly ruined
But just ask
And I'll still choose you.

XI

Regrets.
I never regretted a thing
Until I met you
And until I chose you
Because I know whether it is
Ten days or ten months from now
Whoever I meet or whoever I see
Will remind me of you.
But truth be told,
You, even you,
I never regretted you.

XII

I couldn't fit in a single poem
How much you meant to me
So I filled five books
But you,
You could fit in a word how much I meant
to you.
Sometimes,
It was 'everything'
And sometimes,
It was 'nothing'

XIII

Perhaps, I'll love again
I am most certain you already have
But as much as I am scared of being alone
I am scared of one day waking up
And not having you in my mind
Or you not seeing me in every roller coaster ride
Of me finding a new something old, something blue
And you finding another set of hands to hold on to.
Ten years later, would you still think of me at nights?
Would I still see you in every guy's eyes?

They'll never ever really understand,
Why I no longer kiss or hold hands
Why every 'I love you' is responded with
'As you should'
And the necklace around my neck
Is of a rusted hue.
I tried so hard to fall in love
To have a muse
That now,
I have got you
In my mind
In my soul
In my body.

There are so many lonely night
On which I read our past chats
I laugh and I cry
I cry because I miss you
I miss your voice
Your stupid smile
And flirty remarks
And how much you care.
And I laugh because just as
I am about to call you
I read something so heartbreakingly wrong
That I remember
I was as much of your muse as you were
mine
The only difference was that
You were my poetry
And I?
I was your entertainment.

Five years later, or perhaps sooner, perhaps later,
I'll try to convince myself that he's my first love
I'll erase your existence from my phone
Perhaps even my body, my mind, my soul.
But these books,
They'll always be the proof of the fact
That you'll always be the first one.

It's 2 am
And here I am
Wondering if you're out there
Trying to forget it all just like I am
If you agree every time you hear
You're better off without her
Or if you say it but don't mean it
And it that's true, then I don't believe that.
You stole all my firsts and hung them beside your thirds,
Like a consolation prize in a hall of honours.
I made you whole
Without me, you have no soul.

When your life flashes before your eyes
The moment before you die,
I want to be a part of the clip
Even if it is just a glimpse.
I want you to want to live
Just so you could see me again.
I want you to want to live
So we could have the goodbye we never had.
I want you to want to live
For me.

Curse you for having a name
That is going to haunt me
For the rest of my life
I'll hear it in every street I pry.
Curse you for having a smile
That I can see on every face.
Curse you for having arms
That I can feel in every embrace.
Curse you for loving me
And throwing me away
Leaving me with wounds
That I can feel in every place.

You called me cute
And pulled my cheeks
Like rubbing the fur
Of stray cat that you see.
You never really loved me, no,
And unlike cats, I didn't boast your serotonin,
I went for your dopamine.
And unlike cats, I wasn't your pet,
I made myself your addiction.

You once told me
That if I were to confess my love for you
You'd cry
And not happy tears.
You'd cry because you would know
That you would never be able to love me
back.

True love?
True love kills
It hurts
It stabs you right in the heart
And it kills
True love kills

You try to replace me over and over again
But then you learn
That the soulmate
Is only one.
And you can scour the earth
To find peace
Only to seek it
Within
Me.

I am scared that one day
You'll wake up and ask,
"She who?"
And as much as I want
My wounds to heal,
I don't want time to do that
Cause if it passes, it will pass for you too.
And honestly,
As much as I want to move on,
I don't want the same for you.
Because I am scared
That the only one who saw me for who I
was
Will forget how I looked too.

I call you my ex
Because what word can I ever use
To describe what we ever had?
Best friends, friends with benefits, lovers:
All seem to miss a component
But if there was a phrase made for us
It would be,
'Not meant to be'

Friends with benefits:
I really think we were that
For a brief moment right there.
Until you realized that I was in love with you
And i realized that
You wanted the benefits
But you never wanted to be my friend.

Perhaps we could've been lovers,
We whispered each other promises at
nights
And clung to our memories in our dreams.
We talked like lovers
Acted like lovers parted like lovers...
There was only one thing
Keeping us from being lovers:
Love.

Baat chhide jo meri kahin
Tum usko bhool bataa dena
Lekin wo bhool ho aisi
Jis'se bezaar nahin

PART 3:

TEARS SCREAMING FROM MY SOUL

My muse,
I can't sleep without you

1

Crimson solitude isn't where I bleed alone
It's where you are right there
And my tears are blood
Pouring out of me
And you choose to ignore it
Because I chose you
But it never meant that you chose me

11

Perhaps if I lie and tell myself
In another life we work
I won't think of the endings
We could've had in this one.
But none could've been like this one
Where I can't hate you
But can't love you either
When you miss me
But can't pick my phone either
When we know what we did was wrong
But what was right...
Wouldn't have been right either.

III

They said true love never had an ending
And we assumed because it was forever
So we tried and tried
To change each other into the pieces that fit
To find some sort of peace
Only to realize that
True love never had an ending
Because it didn't exist.

IV

Some days you stare at your wrist a little
more than the others.
Some days your eyes linger on the knife a
moment longer.
Some days you wonder about the colour of
your blood out of more than just
inquisitiveness.
Some days you want to find out about
death out of more than just fearfulness.
There are times when you are walking
down the path
And you are simply deep in a trance
With no idea where it will lead
Just voices whispering in deep
Those are the days you know you beat it
When you have won but know the cycle
will repeat

There's just no way to treat it
It won't go away till you bleed.

I fall asleep, imagining sleeping in your lap,
Pretending that the wind wasn't air, it was your hand
Felt your arms around my body
Wondered if you were watching me as if you were in love with me
The delusion melted soon after,
And suddenly,
The pillow was just cotton,
The wind just breathless,
The blanket just wool,
And realised I couldn't love you.

VI

While saying bye, I wished I had never said hi,
It's not regret, it's remorse,
It's the ashes of my heart, ceaselessly trying to go back in time,
It's the hum in my voice, breaking down at your sight
We made it so far, so far, but that was all
Cause you realised I could never be your forever,
Cause I realized infinity was just too long,
Cause we realized always just wasn't for us.
But how do we smile, how do we pretend it's fine,
When the blood in our veins screams for us
But we are two pieces that could never fit.

VII

They say a true love's kiss makes your heart stop
Or perhaps beat faster
But I remember
With you
It stopped
And began again at such a pace
That I fainted
And you caught me.
I wish I wasn't talking in past tense right now.

VIII

I think it felt so good to be embraced
That we forgot how our skin burned
Not with passion but with hurt
Every time we hugged
Because that was what we were
Two unlovable and unfixable beings
Made of knives
And we left each other bare
Bleeding.

IX

I read somewhere
That if you love someone don't hide
Show your love with a smile
And so I did
Only to remember that I was only good with games
And I don't think you understood anything but that either
So for all those believing in this piece of advice:
Don't.
If you're in love don't show
At least that way he won't crush your soul.

What we had was never love
It was ache and need at best
We could never get the one
So found a replacement
Just to have some fun
We became addicted
Like drugs
But it was worse
It was poison
That killed the two of us

But I don't pick up either

PART 4:

VERSES BLEEDING FROM MY HEART

The stars are extra beautiful tonight probably cause I am watching them with you.

1

There is a brief time after midnight
When I close my eyes
And I wonder, if I am sleeping next to your
ghost.

There is a brief time after midnight
When the temperature drops low
And I feel your eyes piercing my soul.

There is a brief time after midnight
When I am half-conscious
And the conversations I have with you are
almost real.

There's a brief time after midnight
When I am telling you about my day
And I can feel you smile

There is a brief time after midnight
When it's so cold, but a breeze makes me warm
And I wonder if it's you

There's a brief time after midnight
When my tears make my shiver
And the feel of your arms is my only comfort

There's a brief time after midnight
When I am painting you
And it feels like you are sitting right there, holding my hand

There's a brief time after midnight
When the darkness falls
But I feel like you are protecting me from afar

There's a brief time after midnight
When I can hear you whispering
"I am not worth it"

11

Oh, forbidden thought in my head
Thinking about you is a habit
I don't have to make an effort.

On cold nights I imagine being in your arms,
I see you, I hold you in my dreams,
Hoping I don't speak while I sleep.

Your name on my tongue is a privilege
With the sweetest taste

I stretch the first syllable,
Halt,
And pour all my love in the second one

You often asked me why I never used your
name

Your name is a word I could never use carelessly
I hold it in like sour tears brimmed in the eyes

Last night, I dreamed of you
I dreamed of you giving me the goodbye I wanted
I dreamed of a soft peck and an embrace

And I forever caress in my mind
You'll always be there
I'll never forget the way your hand felt in mine

And I'll forever wonder the taste of your lips
The feel of your kiss
And I'll forever regret not being able

To tell you how I felt.
I don't write this out of love,
Or sorrow, or hate, or longing

I write this out of regret
On a cold Tuesday evening
When I need to hear your voice

And no drug or dream
Can give me that
I feel like I am losing you

I feel like one day you'll just be a faded
memory
And I'll be carrying this empty heart
Not being able to remember what it was
filled with

And when I'd try to imagine you,
There'd be no face
No voice
Not touch
Just a feel and one word,

III

When air failed to fill my air sacs,
darkness creeped in my lungs,
slowly crawled into my bronchioles,
and diffused in my blood.
My bulb,
my heart was already fussed,
too weak to resist,
to fight,
to live.
That day,
I succumbed to the darkness.
The stars in my eyes dimmed,
the sun in my veins gave out,
and came the eternal lifeless,
lightless, night.
No moon laid there to help me.

My heart thudded wildly against the cages
as the poison of darkness slowly seeped
into it
and killed it mercilessly.
My heart,
once a garden,
became a dungeon,
the darkest of all.
And I was reduced to a mere intransigent
jailor.

That sinking feeling
when all your emotions
rush in
when your eyes
finally open
and you realise she wasn't imaginary at all
and that you pushed her too far
is when you realize
that you did love her.

I pity the clouds
Always lifelessly floating above
With only one purpose in their life:
To fall.

I
feel
like
a cloud.

Some fears go away after a while.
Some haunt you for your life.
And some reside and just don't leave you.
Ever.

Those first start as panic, become phobias
and then
they become instincts.

Instincts.

Those are the worst.

So bad that your mind doesn't even have to
think.
They become stimuli.

Your brain forgets.
Your body remembers.
Your muscles remember.

Your soul
does
not forget.

Those are the worst kind of fears.

You can lie to your brain
Your body
Your heart.

But
how
do
you
lie
to your soul
if you don't remember
what you were afraid of?

VII

I
can't
fight
anymore.

My heart is stiched together.
My scars are taped.
My bones are glued.

But
they
are
still
broken
and torn.

My
soul
still
remembers.

My eyes replay the horrific memories of my past battles.
My nose winces everytime I see my weapons.
My face grimaces everytime my body wills to fight

The memories haunt me.
I can't prepare for battles anymore.
Cause the blood in my veins still screams.

VIII

Every
cell
fights
the
urge
to not let go.

IX

Trauma doesn't let me play anymore
How do I try to hurt someone
If my flesh is ripped
and my broken bones are my knives.

How do I try to play
If my weavers have pulled
my scarf
to an end.

The nib of my pen screeches.
Its lifeforce if waning.

I wonder,
Do I sound like that?

XI

Do you tell yourself
That it was my fault
That I was unstable
Jumped off cause
Cause I wasn't sustainable
Too weak, too frail
Trust me, too emotional.

Is that what you tell yourself?
What do you tell yourself?

Do you tell yourself
It's better now
Now that I wiped out
My existence
Cause I wasn't meant for you

Too sweet, too naïve
Trust me, too bright.

Is that what you tell yourself?
What do you tell yourself?

So what do you tell yourself
On blue nights
When the dark sky
Hunts the moonlight
Did you find youself
A star to love
Or are you still hung
Over the moon gone?

So I told myself
What you wanted me to do
Slit the fabric
Of the suit
And did you like me
In the glistening red
Or did you want the angel back?

But isn't that what you told me to do?
What did you want me to do?

XII

I fell for your butter
You were easy to get
Hard to hold on to.

XIII

I don't know what to do
I am at a crossroads
I am standing
I am staring
I am tired, I want to turn back
I am sick, I am suffocated
I can't do this anymore,
The façade's too heavy
It's draining me
My feet are sore
I have come so far
But I can't go on
I want to lie down
I want to take a deep breath and relax
But I push myself onto the road
That demands more
Grated with thorns

It has a thick poisonous sheet for air
It is killing me
Slowly, efficiently
But I don't want to live any longer
So when the end came
It's long awaited
I want it, I craze it
I need it.
And so, I let the angel carry me to other
side
And she puts me again in front of a
crossroads
And just as every cycle goes,
I again choose the same path
And this time hoping for love.

At times, when I lay on my bed
Staring at the wooden ceiling
And my bed's creaking
And I am not sleeping
I wonder if
You lied when you said that you didn't love me
Or lied when you confessed
I wonder if
You lied when you said that you trusted me
Or lied when you didn't tell
You've got me struggling
So many lies, so many times
And when I stare at your back
Before everything goes black
I wonder if
You lied when you said you didn't miss me
Or lied every time you called

I wonder if
The signs were so ugly
That even I ignored them
And comes the sunrise
I never said I loved you
Until you didn't
But when we fall back remembering
I wonder if
You lied when you said you're good
Or lied when you said you wanted me
And the day's ours, sweetheart
But that's it
Cause you'll depart
And I'll start
Craving your heart
Wondering
If you lied when you said you didn't love me
Or lied when you confessed
Wondering if you had any idea how much
you hurt me
Or how I was depressed.

Can I tell a story through this song?
About how two lovers couldn't sing along.
Can I tell a story through this song?
About how two lovers couldn't sing along

It all started when we were both young,
At a campfire where old songs were sung.
We were two silly kids not knowing about love,
Just goofing around standing in awe of,
One another
Oh we were amazed by 'one another'

Fishing with our dads,
Tennis with our moms
We never liked the sports
Just the reason to come

Passing chits in class
Making fun of one other
But now,
I want to tell a story through this song
About how two lovers couldn't sing along.

You were my childhood sweetheart
Until life pulled us apart
Ended at different ends of the world
Without each other, we were both struck
Dead
Yeah apart we were just dead

I don't know if I am in love
But you're all that I think of
I can't sleep without you
But I don't pick up either (Yeah I don't pick up your phone)
You must think that I am over the past
But boy oh how can I even last (I can't last)
Without you

Can you hear our story through this song?
About how we couldn't sing along.

I will love you in my memories
I'll love you when I am in the shower or listening to that song
I will love you when I think of my birthday and the cake that you bought
I'll love you when u reminisce the fireworks and the way my hand you held

I'll miss you when i think about the way you kissed my forehead
I'll miss you when i need that tight embrace
I'll miss you when i recount the smell of your perfume
I'll miss you when there's no one to make innuendoes.

But I'll never love or miss you more than when you're right there, but there's a hollow in your heart's place, and there're no memories enough to make us care.

XVII

I held on to you,
Even after your heart stopped beating for me,
I held on to you,
Even as your face became a painful reminder of what I could never have.
I held on to you,
Even when it physically hurt to look at you.
I held on to you,
Even as I saw you fall in love with her.
I held on to you,
As I saw you find everything I could never be.
I held on to you,
When you broke all your rules for her.
I held on to you,
Even though I had to let go of myself in the process.

No matter how hard I try,
You are the last thought I have before drifting off.
No matter how hard I try,
You are the first reminder in the morning.
No matter how hard I try,
I still can't resist answering to all your texts.
No matter how hard I try,
I can't convince myself to hate you.

I have all my friends,
All people who aren't toxic,
Who treat me right,
Who love me,
But when I am hugging myself, sobbing,
There's no one but you that I want there,
Even if you're the reason I am crying.

The water is so fragile
One single touch and it breaks.

The water is so strong
It fixes itself right after.

Don't erase my scars,
Love them.
Don't heal me,
Fall for me broken.
Don't patch me up,
Hold me as I bandage myself.
Don't worry about me being lonely,
Just leave me enough good memories to
reminisce when you are gone.
Don't protect me from others,
Hand me a knife, I can fight.
No need to put yourself in front of the gun,
Be there for me, I'll survive.
Don't pity me, I am not broken,
Help me become a survivor.
Don't grow my wings,
Help me take off.
Don't try to make me better,
Treat me like I am the best.

I am unoxidated
So damn intoxicated
My impulses are gone
My instincts were never strong
And now

I breath oxide
My mind tells lies
My soul is always wandering
It leaves me wondering
Am I living ghost
Am I all but a shadow
Have my demons taken control
How am I so shallow

How does my heart still beat
When I don't feel

And my brain succumbs to
The urge to let go

Am I living ghost
Am I all but a shadow
Have my demons taken control
How am I so shallow
I feel like a living ghost...

There is a silence in my mind
I can't leave anything behind
I am bound to this place
I haunt this body
Trapped in a cage
But nobody's sorry

Cause they got me here
They took their symbols and
They got me here
With their holy books
They struck me here
With those empty prayers
They locked me here

It was them
And they try to kill me
Tying me up, burning me down
Chocking me up, drowning me down
But they don’t understand that
I am already dead

I am a living ghost
With my demons in control
I am a mere shadow
Oh so damn shallow

See a harshly torn tee shirt
Tear it down properly
And take a needly and cover up the small
holes
And make the food stains look like blobs of
pain

Take up some stickers the smile's too grim
Some glitter, the shine's too dim
Said don't make it too shiny
Don't let it hide my glam
Just make it bright enough to meet my
grades

And when you were done smiling at the
cameras with it
It went to the dumpster behind the hill

You were always good with DIY
Fixed up everything that caught your eye
Made me think I was attractive
When I was actually unwanted
You were always good with DIY

See a harshly torn tee shirt
Tear it down properly
And take a needly and cover up the small holes
And make the food stains look like blobs of pain

Take up some stickers the smile's too grim
Some glitter, the shine's too dim
Said don't make it too shiny
Don't let it hide my glam
Just make it bright enough to meet my grades

And when you were done smiling at the cameras with it
It went to the dumpster behind the hill

The stars are extra beautiful tonight probably cause you're one of them.

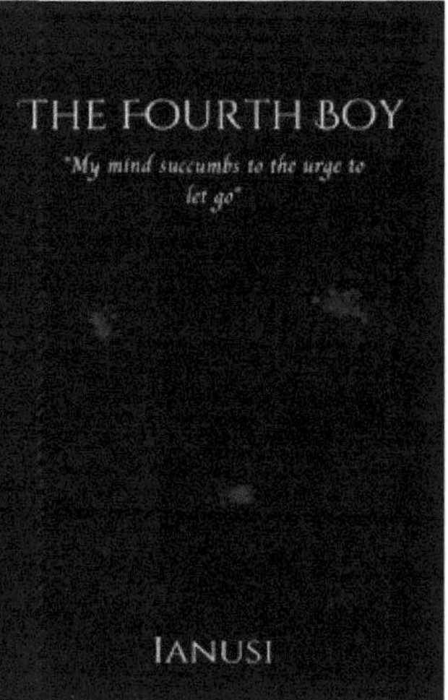
THE FOURTH BOY
"My mind succumbs to the urge to let go"
IANUSI

INTRANSIGENT THOUGHTS
Ianusi

VEILED DREAMS
Ianusi

CRIMSON SOLITUDE
Ianusi

VENTURES OF GEM LAND
The Black Time
JANUSHI RAICHURA

VENTURES OF GEM LAND
The Banished Heretics

VENTURES OF GEM LAND
The Alchemic Presage
JANUSHI RAICHURA

VENTURES OF GEM LAND
The Gorgon's Curse
JANUSHI RAICHURA

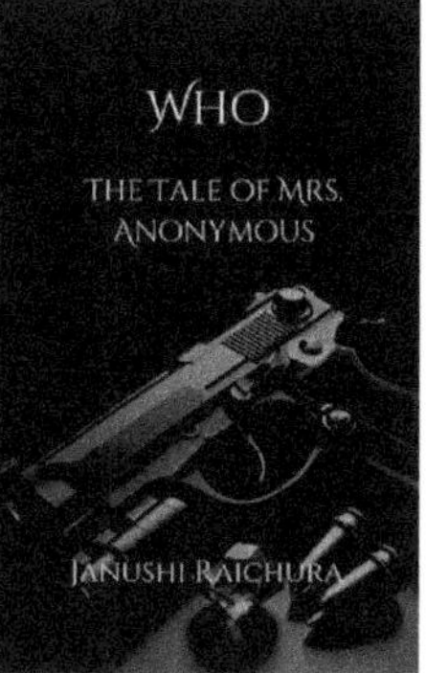
WHO
THE TALE OF MRS. ANONYMOUS
JANUSHI RAICHURA

WHO-2
THE ENFORCEMEN OF YOUTH ESPIONAGE
JANUSHI RAICHURA

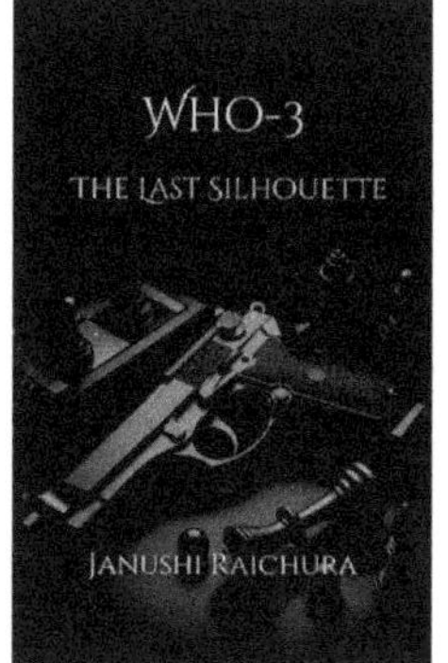
WHO-3
THE LAST SILHOUETTE
JANUSHI RAICHURA

CRYPTIC PASSIONS
JANUSHI RAICHURA

HACKING AFFECTIONS
JANUSHI RAICHURA

My Soul's Verses
Janushi

The Hues of Samsara
Janushi Raichura

Be A TWF
THE PRISMATIC ELEVEN
Chief Editor
JANUSHI RAICHURA

BONDS OF MIDNIGHT

www.ingramcontent.com/pod-product-compliance
Lightning Source LLC
LaVergne TN
LVHW021159160826
845679LV00024B/2162